Up and Away

Text: Robert Coupe

Consultant: Richard Wood, Curator, Powerhouse Museum, Sydney

This edition first published 2003 by

MASON CREST PUBLISHERS INC.

370 Reed Road

Broomall, PA 19008

© Weldon Owen Inc.

Conceived and produced by

Weldon Owen Pty Limited

Library of Congress Cataloging-in-Publication Data

on file at the Library of Congress

ISBN: 1-59084-184-0

Printed in Singapore.

1 2 3 4 5 6 7 8 9 06 05 04 03

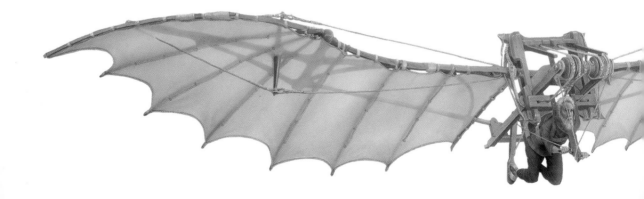

CONTENTS

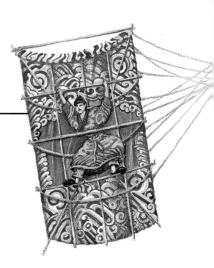

LEGENDS

People have always wanted to fly. The ancient Greeks had many myths and legends about flying. One was about a flying horse, called Pegasus, that carried a warrior through the air to help him find and kill an evil monster. Another Greek myth was about a boy called Icarus who flew too close to the Sun.

Icarus
Icarus and his father used wax to stick wings to their arms. When Icarus flew close to the Sun, the wax melted and he fell to the ground.

Vishnu is an Indian god of the Hindu religion. When he wanted to fly across the sky, he rode on the back of a huge bird, called a garuda. Indonesia named its national airline "Garuda" after this bird.

Getting a Lift

Birds have hollow bones, which make them light, but if it weren't for the special shape of their wings, they would sink to the ground. When a bird is flying, air flows over its outstretched wings. The air that goes underneath the wing flows more slowly than the air that goes over the curved top. The slow-moving air under the wings is thicker. It pushes the bird upward and keeps it in the air.

Lift Off
Like a plane taking off, a swan needs to gain more and more speed until it is going fast enough to rise into the air.

This boat is called a hydrofoil. It has underwater wings like the wings of a plane. When the hydrofoil goes very fast, the wings lift the boat clear of the water so that it skims across the surface.

Flying Paper

Hold a piece of thin paper in front of your mouth. Blow hard across the top, and watch it lift up, just like when air flows over the wing of a bird or an airplane.

Formation Flying
This flock of geese is flying in a V-formation, with one bird at the front and the others trailing behind to the left and right.

Flocks of geese fly long distances in a V-formation. As the bird in front flaps its wings, it sends air back over the wings of the birds behind. The other birds do not have to flap their wings as hard, and can save energy for the long flight. When the front bird gets tired, it moves to the back and another one takes its place.

Wing Cutaway
Look closely at the shape of this seagull's wing. Compare it with the airplane wing opposite.

Shapes and Sizes

Some birds, like albatrosses and condors, have wings that help them fly long distances using strong currents of air. The wings of many smaller birds, such as swifts, quails, and sparrows, are better for flying shorter distances. A hummingbird's short, narrow wings allow it to hover in the air like a helicopter as it flaps them quickly in circles. You can tell a lot about the way a bird flies by looking at the shape and size of its wings.

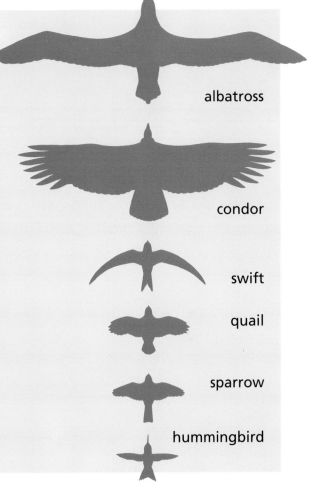

albatross

condor

swift

quail

sparrow

hummingbird

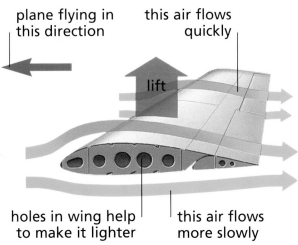

plane flying in this direction

this air flows quickly

lift

holes in wing help to make it lighter

this air flows more slowly

Air Flow and Lift

Just like a bird's wing, an airplane's wing is shaped so that air flows over it very quickly, and under it more slowly. The air flow helps push it upward. We call this upward pressure "lift."

9

Warm Currents

When warm air near the ground moves upward, large birds, such as vultures, can ride on the moving air currents without using much energy.

Going Up

When winds blow against a hill or cliff, the air is forced upward, giving birds a free ride.

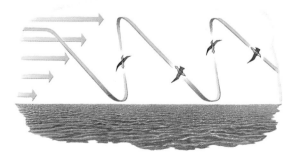

Ocean Winds

Albatrosses use their outstretched wings to ride on winds that blow over the oceans.

STRANGE BUT TRUE

Some fish can fly, but not very far. Flying fish push themselves out of the water by lashing their tails at a great speed. They have very wide fins that stretch out to help them glide through the air.

Birds are not the only animals that can move through the air. Some mammals that live in forests have built-in parachutes. This flying squirrel has wide flaps of skin between its paws. It can glide on currents of air from one tree to the next by stretching out its paws. The flaps of skin catch the air underneath.

Insects are the smallest animals that can fly. While a bird has only one pair of wings, many insects have two pairs. Bats are also flying animals, but they are mammals, not birds. Their wings are made of skin that stretches back from their arms and fingers.

Bat Flight
The bones in a bat's wings stretch out the flaps of skin it uses to fly.

DID YOU KNOW?

Watch a honeybee hovering around a flower. You probably won't be able to see its wings because they are flapping too fast to see. Look at other insects and see how rapidly they move their wings. The smaller the insect, the faster it flaps its wings.

DRAGONFLY

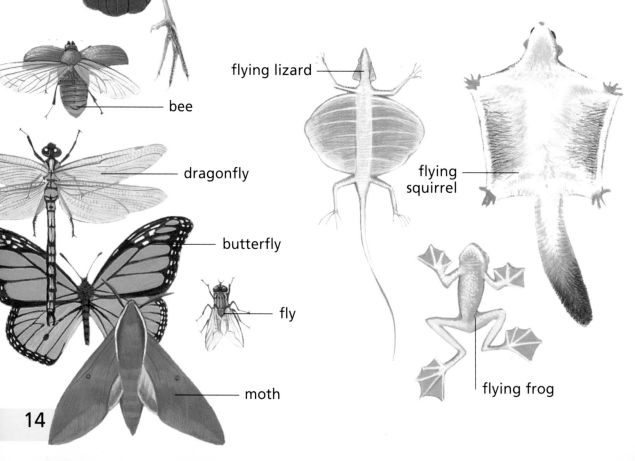

vulture's wing
spread wide

moorhen

hummingbird

Spreading Out

The three animals below are not true fliers. They take off by jumping and then glide by spreading their body out wide.

bee

flying lizard

flying
squirrel

dragonfly

butterfly

fly

moth

flying frog

Different flying animals use the shape of their body to fly in different ways. Birds flap their wings to take off from the ground and to push themselves up and forward. Birds can also float or glide on currents and winds. Insects have to flap their wings all the time to stay in the air and cannot glide. Other flying animals do not have wings to lift them into the air, but glide down from high places until they land.

Ancient and Modern
The animal above is a pterosaur. Pterosaurs were flying reptiles that lived from more than 200 million years ago until 63 million years ago. Like bats, below, they had wings made of skin that they flapped by moving their bony arms.

Crowd Pleaser
Kites were very popular in ancient Japan. Crowds would gather to admire their wonderful colors.

FLYING KITES

People first figured out how to make and fly kites almost 2,500 years ago. In ancient China, they made kites of silk and bamboo. Later, people used paper. These kites were often large and colorful. Sometimes kites were in the shape of dragons and other animals in Chinese legends.

Stories from ancient China say that men were sent up in huge kites in times of war. Their job was to find out where the enemy armies were. They may have been the first people to fly—more than 2,000 years ago!

More than 100 years ago, an Australian named Lawrence Hargrave tried to build a flying machine. He did not succeed, but he did invent a new kind of kite, called a box kite. In 1894 he tied four box kites together with ropes. He held on to one of the kites, and a strong wind carried him and the kites 16 feet (5 meters) up into the air.

Is It a Bird?
No, it's a kite! But this kite flies just as an albatross or a large eagle does when it uses its large wings to ride on the wind.

Aircraft Design
Early airplanes used box kites for wings. They had two sets of wings, one above the other.

MAKE YOUR OWN KITE

What you need
- 2 thin sticks, one about 2 ft. (60 cm) and the other 1½ ft. (45 cm)
- 1 sheet of thick paper
- 11 yards (10 m) string
- glue
- strips of fabric

1 Tie two sticks together to make a cross shape. This is the frame of your kite.

2 Cut a sheet of paper into a diamond shape, a little wider and longer than the cross.

3 Fold the edges of the paper over and glue the diamond shape onto the cross.

4 Cut a piece of string 15 inches (40 cm) long. Make two holes in the center of the kite and pass the string through to make a loop. Tie the ends of the string together. Tie the rest of the string to this loop. This is your flying string.

5 Tie strips of fabric to the bottom corner of your kite to make a tail. This will help your kite to fly more evenly. Now paint your kite.

Step one

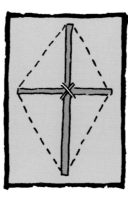

Step two

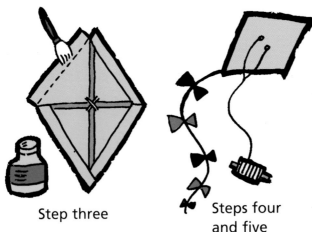

Step three

Steps four and five

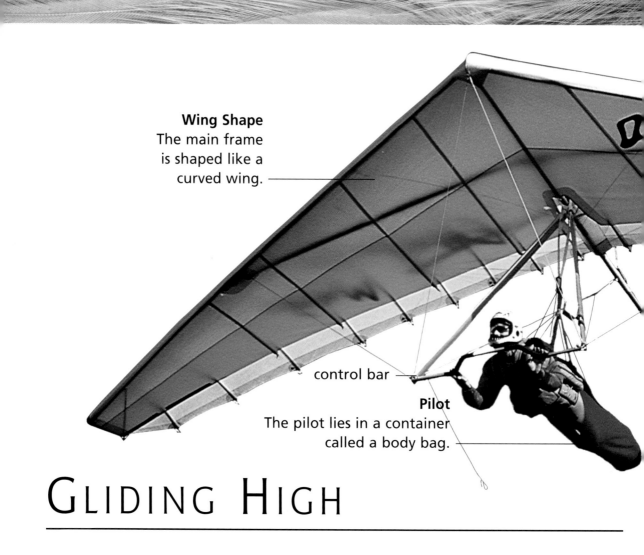

Wing Shape
The main frame
is shaped like a
curved wing.

control bar

Pilot
The pilot lies in a container
called a body bag.

GLIDING HIGH

A hang glider is like a large, strong, and very complicated kite. A glider pilot usually begins a flight from a high cliff or ridge. Like a kite, a standard hang glider does not have an engine. It sails along on currents of air until it glides back down to the ground. Pilots direct gliders with the control bar and by moving the weight of their own body.

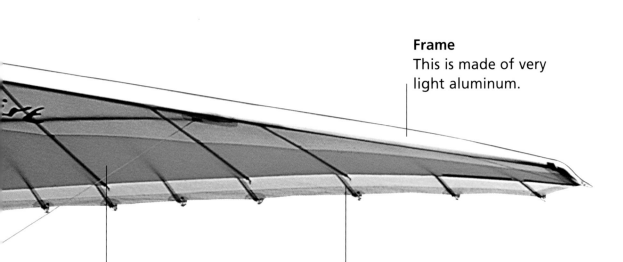

Frame
This is made of very light aluminum.

Rip-proof Wing
This is made of light, strong nylon that won't tear.

Battens
These are curved so that air flows more slowly under than over the frame.

Going Up

To climb, the pilot pushes the control bar forward. This pushes the front of the glider up.

Going Down

To dive, the pilot pulls the control bar back. The top of the glider then slopes down.

Going Sideways

To move to the left or right, the pilot moves in that direction.

Compare Leonardo da Vinci's flying machine with the picture of a hang glider on page 20. Notice how alike the two pictures are.

Leonardo da Vinci was a famous artist who lived almost 500 years ago. Leonardo was also a great inventor. He believed that people would one day be able to fly. He did not create a flying machine, but he did dream up the idea of a machine with wings that flapped like a bird's.

MAKE YOUR OWN GLIDER

What you need
- a piece of cardboard
- a pencil
- a pair of scissors
- clay

1 Fold a piece of cardboard in half. Draw half a glider, as shown.

2 With the cardboard still folded, cut around your drawing. Now unfold the cardboard.

3 Stick a small piece of clay underneath the glider's nose. Throw it gently forward, and it will glide through the air.

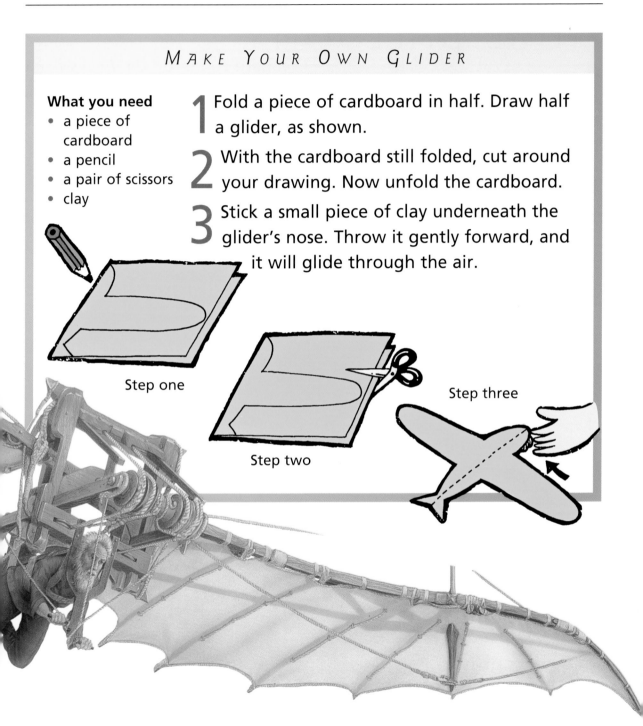

Step one

Step two

Step three

Huge Balloons

Before there were passenger planes, people flew long distances in huge airships. Airships were like sausage-shaped balloons. Inside a rigid frame, early airships contained bags of a gas called hydrogen, which is lighter than air, and were driven by powerful engines. Later, a safer gas called helium was used.

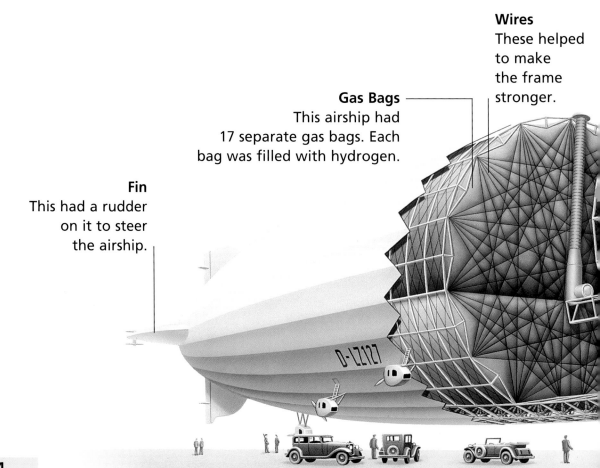

Wires
These helped to make the frame stronger.

Gas Bags
This airship had 17 separate gas bags. Each bag was filled with hydrogen.

Fin
This had a rudder on it to steer the airship.

D-LZ127

Traveling in Comfort

Passengers traveled in a cabin, called a gondola, beneath the airship. This is a view from above the gondola of an airship that flew between America and Europe from 1928 to 1937.

bathrooms | sleeping cabins | living room/ dining room | radio room

washroom | galley | control

Frame
The frame of the airship was made of lightweight metal.

Covering
The frame was covered with a light, painted fabric.

RAF ZEPPELIN

Flying Advertisements

Modern airships look much like the airships of more than 70 years ago, but they are filled with helium, which cannot burn. They often take passengers on sightseeing trips.

In May 1937, the hydrogen inside one of the world's largest airships, the *Hindenburg*, exploded as it landed in New Jersey. Thirty-five of the 97 people on board were killed. After that, there were no more long passenger flights on airships. Before the destruction of the *Hindenburg*, airships had been used for many different purposes other than passenger flights.

USS *Macon*
This was built in 1933. It belonged to
the US Navy.

Graf Zeppelin
This began flights across the Atlantic
Ocean in 1928. It carried 20 passengers.

R-34
In 1919, this
became the first
airship to fly
across the
Atlantic.

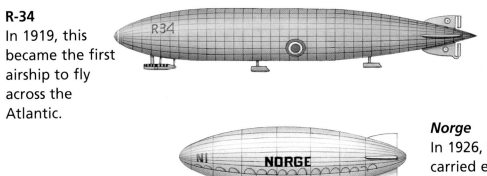

Norge
In 1926, this airship
carried explorers to
the North Pole.

Boeing 747-400
This is a modern
passenger jet. It can carry
20 times as many
passengers as the *Graf
Zeppelin* did, but it does
not have sleeping cabins.

Santos-Dumont
In 1901, a Brazilian named
Alberto Santos-Dumont flew
around the Eiffel Tower in
Paris in this tiny airship.

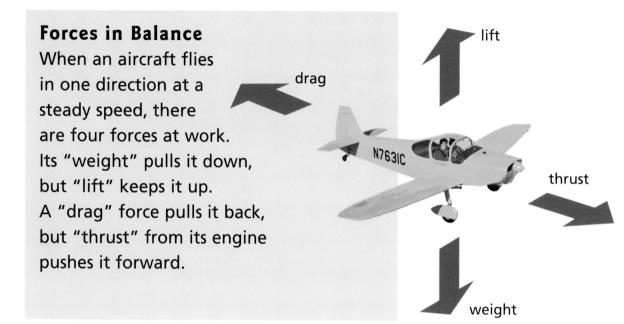

Forces in Balance

When an aircraft flies in one direction at a steady speed, there are four forces at work. Its "weight" pulls it down, but "lift" keeps it up. A "drag" force pulls it back, but "thrust" from its engine pushes it forward.

lift

drag

thrust

weight

FLYING AN AIRCRAFT

Like birds and kites and gliders, an aircraft is heavier than air. To stay in the air, it needs to keep moving forward. Its engine provides the thrust that moves it along. The air that flows beneath its curved wings gives it the lift that keeps it from falling. An aircraft has parts on its wings and tail that the pilot can move to make the plane change direction.

elevators

Going Up

Underneath its tail an aircraft has elevators. These go up to make the plane rise. They go down to make it descend.

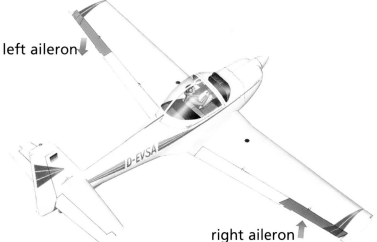
left aileron

right aileron

Bending (Banking)

Behind the end of each wing is an aileron. The pilot moves these up or down to make the plane tilt to one side or the other.

rudder

Right Turn

When the rudder turns right, the nose of the plane also turns right.

GLOSSARY

ailerons Movable parts at the end of a plane's wings. These go up or down to make the plane tilt to the left or right.

battens Thin strips of wood or metal that strengthen the wings of hang gliders.

elevators Movable parts of a plane's tail that go up or down to make the plane go higher or lower.

fin The vertical part of an airplane's or an airship's tail, which does not move. It helps keep the plane or airship steady.

gliders Animals that have wide flaps of skin that they stretch out to ride on air currents as they glide for short distances, usually between trees.

hang glider A flying machine that is controlled by a pilot, who hangs beneath its wings. It has no engines, but flies by gliding on currents of air.

hydrofoil A boat that is lifted above the water by wings or foils beneath its hull.

mammal An animal that grows inside its mother's body before it is born. The young drink their mother's milk.

reptiles Cold-blooded animals that have backbones and dry skin covered by scales or a hard shell.

rudder A movable control that changes the plane's direction.

INDEX

PICTURE AND ILLUSTRATION CREDITS

BOOKS IN THIS SERIES